AF413314

SECRET OF SOLOPRENEUR'S ODYSSEY

NAVIGATING THE PATH TO SELF-EMPLOYMENT

DR. MINAKSHI BANSAL

To all the dreamers, the doers, and the daring souls who dare to forge their own paths.

ᗒᗒᗒ

Contents

Prayer   *vii*

About The Author   *ix*

Preface   *xiii*

1. The Spark Within: Discovering Your Entrepreneurial Passion   1

Part 1

2. Leap Of Faith: Overcoming Fears And Embracing Uncertainty 7

Part 2

3. Blueprint For Dreams: Crafting Your Business Plan   13

Part 3

4. Solo, But Not Alone: Building A Support Network   19

Part 4

5. Mastering The Juggle: Balancing Work And Life   25

Part 5

6. Money Matters: Financial Planning For Solopreneurs   31

Part 6

7. Marketing Mojo: Attracting And Engaging Clients   37

Part 7

8. Tech Toolkit: Essential Tools For Digital Success   43

Part 8

9. Client Whisperer: Building Strong Relationships   49

Part 9

10. Resilience Roadmap: Bouncing Back From Setbacks   55

Part 10

11. Growth Mindset: Cultivating A Thirst For Learning   61

Part 11

12. The Solopreneur's Brand: Creating Your Unique Identity   67

Contents

Part 12

13. Productivity Power-Ups: Optimizing Your Workflow   73

Part 13

14. Legal Landscape: Understanding Contracts And Compliance 79

Part 14

15. Taxes Demystified: Simplifying Finances For Solopreneurs 85

Part 15

16. The Art Of Delegation: Knowing When To Outsource   91

Part 16

17. The Solopreneur's Sanctuary: Designing Your Ideal Workspace 97

Part 17

18. The Power Of Community: Connecting With Fellow   103
    Solopreneurs

Part 18

19. Celebrating Milestones: Acknowledging Your Successes   109

Part 19

20. The Ever-Evolving Journey: Embracing Change And   115
    Continued Growth

Part 20

21. Summary   121

Citation and References   127

Other Books of The Author   129

Prayer

"Om Poornamadah Poornamidam Poornaat Poornamudachyate,
Poornasya Poornamaadaya Poornamevavashishyate"
"Om Shantih, Shantih, Shantih"

*The literal interpretation of this mantra is: That which is Absolute,
This which is Absolute, Absolute arises from Absolute, If Absolute is
removed from Absolute, Absolute remains*

*This mantra is a reminder of the fundamental truth that all of
existence is rooted in the Absolute. It is a reminder that the Absolute is
the source of all that is, and that it is ever-present, even when all else
is taken away. It is a reminder of the peace that comes from
understanding and accepting this truth.*
Om Peace, Peace, Peace.

ॐॐॐ

About The Author

Dr. Minakshi Bansal, born in the bustling metropolis of Delhi, India, has led a life steeped in artistry, scholarly pursuit, and an unwavering commitment to societal betterment. Following her marriage, she relocated to Ahmedabad, Gujarat, where she has since blossomed into a multifaceted beacon of inspiration for many. Dr. Minakshi is not only recognized as a gifted artist in the realm of Fine Arts but also as an esteemed author, a devoted social worker and a dedicated research scholar in Psychology. Her journey, marked by a profound dedication to elevating those around her, especially the downtrodden and underprivileged children of society, is a testament to her deep-seated belief in the transformative power of engagement and empathy.

From her earliest days, Minakshi was distinguished by an insatiable appetite for reading. Her literary universe was inhabited by characters and narratives that spanned ethical tales, motivational and inspirational stories, and the mythic parables imbued with life lessons. This voracious reading habit was not merely for personal edification but was driven by a desire to distill and disseminate the essence of these narratives to foster the development of students and peers alike. She was particularly captivated by the lives and teachings of historical figures and spiritual leaders such as Adi Shankaracharya, Swami Vivekananda, Dr. APJ Abdul Kalam, Mahamana Pandit Madan Mohan Malviya, Mahatma Gandhi, Sardar Vallabhai Patel, and Vinoba Bhave, among others. Their philosophies and life stories fueled her ambition to embody their ideals of resilience, selflessness, and relentless pursuit of knowledge.

Dr. Minakshi's academic and practical engagement with psychology has been equally noteworthy. As a research scholar, her focus has been on exploring the intricate tapestry of the human psyche, aiming to unlock the potential for psychological well-being and societal harmony. Her scholarly work is complemented by her active involvement in social work, where she employs her academic insights to make tangible differences in the lives of the underprivileged. Her endeavours in social work are characterized by an innovative approach that combines traditional wisdom with contemporary psychological practices to address the multifaceted challenges faced by these communities.

Her artistic talents, another facet of her diverse capabilities, are not merely a personal passion but also serve as a medium through which she communicates and connects with others. Her art, rich in symbolism and emotional depth, reflects her philosophical inquiries and social concerns, offering viewers a glimpse into the breadth of her intellect and the depth of her compassion.

In addition to her contributions to the arts and social sciences, Dr. Minakshi has embraced the healing arts of Pranic Healing, mastering the techniques developed by Master Choa Kok Sui. This practice, which focuses on the manipulation of Prana or life energy to heal the body and aura, has been both a personal journey of discovery and a means through which she extends her healing touch to others. Her proficiency in Pranic Healing is complemented by her advocacy and teaching of various forms of meditation aimed at rejuvenation, personal betterment, and the cultivation of harmony within individuals and communities alike.

Dr. Minakshi's life is a narrative of relentless pursuit, not just of personal achievement but of the upliftment and empowerment of society at large. Her diverse interests and talents—spanning the arts, literature, psychology, and the healing practices—converge on a singular path of service. She embodies the spirit of the luminaries who inspired her, channelling their legacy through her actions and teachings. Through her books, art, and social initiatives, she continues to inspire a new generation to embark on their own journeys of self-discovery, resilience, and altruism.

Her commitment to social betterment, particularly her focus on uplifting underprivileged children, reflects a deep understanding of the transformative potential of education and personal development. By integrating her knowledge of psychology, her artistic sensibilities, and her healing practices, Dr. Bansal has developed a holistic approach to social work that addresses both the immediate needs and the long-term well-being of the communities she serves.

As an author, Dr. Minakshi's writings offer a blend of inspirational insights, practical wisdom, and reflective contemplations drawn from her extensive reading and life experiences. Her books serve as a guide for those seeking to navigate the complexities of life with grace, resilience, and purpose. Through her narratives, she extends an invitation to her readers to explore the depths of their own potential and to contribute meaningfully to the collective well-being of society.

In Dr. Minakshi Bansal, we find a remarkable synthesis of the artist, the scholar, the healer, and the social activist. Her life's work stands as a beacon of hope and a source of inspiration for individuals seeking to make a difference in the world. Her story is a compelling reminder of the power of individual action, rooted in compassion and driven by a profound commitment to the betterment of humanity. Dr. Minakshi's legacy is not just in the tangible outcomes of her efforts but in the enduring spirit of inquiry, empathy, and service that she embodies.

Preface

In the tapestry of my life, the threads of entrepreneurship have always shimmered brightly. As a young girl, I was captivated by the stories of trailblazers who dared to forge their own paths, building businesses from the ground up and leaving their mark on the world. I was inspired by their courage, their creativity, and their unwavering belief in themselves.

As I embarked on my own career, I found myself drawn to the world of solopreneurship. The allure of autonomy, the freedom to pursue my passions, and the opportunity to create something meaningful were irresistible. But as I ventured into the uncharted territory of self-employment, I quickly realized that it was not a path for the faint of heart. It was a journey filled with challenges, setbacks, and moments of self-doubt.

Yet, it was also a journey of immense growth, learning, and transformation. Through trial and error, mentorship, and sheer determination, I navigated the complexities of building a business, cultivating a loyal clientele, and balancing the demands of work and life. Along the way, I discovered valuable lessons, unearthed hidden strengths, and forged meaningful connections with fellow solopreneurs.

This book is a culmination of my experiences, insights, and lessons learned on the winding road of solopreneurship. It's a guidebook for those who dare to dream, who yearn for autonomy, and who seek to build a life and career on their own terms. It's a testament to the power of passion, resilience, and the unwavering belief in one's own potential.

Within these pages, you'll find practical advice, real-world examples, and actionable strategies for navigating the path to self-employment. You'll learn how to identify your entrepreneurial passion, overcome fears, craft a business plan, build a strong brand, market your services, manage your finances, and create a sustainable work-life balance. You'll also discover the power of community, the importance of mentorship, and the transformative potential of continuous learning and growth.

This book is not a magic formula for instant success. It's a roadmap, a guide, a companion on your journey. It's a reminder that you're not alone, that there are countless others who have walked this path before you, and that with the right mindset, tools, and support, you can achieve your dreams.

Whether you're a budding entrepreneur with a burning desire to start your own business or a seasoned solopreneur looking to refine your skills and expand your reach, this book is for you. It's a celebration of the solopreneur spirit, a testament to the power of human ingenuity, and an invitation to embark on an extraordinary journey of self-discovery, growth, and fulfillment.

So, open your mind, embrace the challenges, and let your passion guide you. The solopreneur's odyssey awaits, and it's yours for the taking.

Dr. Minakshi Bansal
Social Activist
Ahmedabad, Gujarat, Bharat

ᗡᗡᗡ

ONE

THE SPARK WITHIN: DISCOVERING YOUR ENTREPRENEURIAL PASSION

The path to solopreneurship is paved with passion. It's a fire that ignites from within, fueled by an unwavering belief in one's ideas and a relentless drive to turn dreams into reality. The journey begins with a spark, a moment of clarity that reveals your true calling. Discovering your entrepreneurial passion is not always a straightforward process; it's a personal odyssey filled with introspection, exploration, and self-discovery.

Often, passion is intertwined with our interests and hobbies. What activities make your heart race? What do you find yourself daydreaming about? Your passions are often hidden in plain sight, woven into the fabric of your everyday life. Reflecting on your past experiences, both personal and professional, can offer valuable clues. What challenges did you overcome? What skills did you develop? Perhaps a past project sparked a new interest or a previous role revealed untapped potential. Don't be afraid to delve deep into your memories and uncover the moments that ignited your curiosity and fueled your ambitions.

Exploration is key to uncovering your passion. Step outside your comfort zone and try new things. Attend workshops, conferences, or online courses that pique your interest. Read books, listen to podcasts, and engage with thought leaders in fields that fascinate you. The more you expose yourself to different ideas and perspectives, the clearer your own path will become. Sometimes, passion lies at the intersection of multiple interests. Embrace your diverse passions and explore how they can be woven together to create a unique and fulfilling entrepreneurial venture.

Self-discovery is an ongoing process that requires both introspection and action. Take the time to understand your values, strengths, and weaknesses. What are you truly passionate about? What impact do you want to make on the world? Answering these questions will help you identify the kind of work that will bring you both personal and professional fulfillment. Don't be afraid to experiment and try different paths. The journey to entrepreneurship is not always linear; it's a winding road filled with unexpected twists and turns. Embrace the uncertainty and allow yourself to evolve as you discover new passions and uncover hidden talents.

The spark of passion is often accompanied by a sense of purpose. When you're truly passionate about something, it goes beyond simply enjoying the activity; it becomes a driving force that compels you to take action. Your passion gives your work meaning and infuses it with a sense of purpose that transcends financial gain. It's this sense of purpose that will sustain you through the challenges and setbacks that inevitably arise on the path to solopreneurship.

The solopreneur's journey is not for the faint of heart. It requires courage, resilience, and an unwavering belief in one's self. But for those who dare to follow their passion, the rewards are immeasurable. A life fueled by passion is a life filled with joy, fulfillment, and the satisfaction of making a meaningful contribution to the world.

Remember, your entrepreneurial passion is unique to you. It's a reflection of your individual experiences, interests, and values. Don't compare yourself to others or feel pressured to follow a path that doesn't resonate with your heart. Trust your instincts, embrace your quirks, and allow your passion to guide you towards a fulfilling and successful entrepreneurial journey.

Discovering your entrepreneurial passion is the first step towards a rewarding and impactful solopreneur career. It's a journey of self-discovery that requires introspection, exploration, and a willingness to embrace uncertainty. But for those who dare to follow their passion, the rewards are immeasurable. A life fueled by passion is a life filled with joy, fulfillment, and the satisfaction of making a meaningful contribution to the world. So, ignite your spark, embrace your journey, and let your passion light the way towards a fulfilling and successful solopreneur odyssey.

ppp

The spark within you is your greatest asset. Nurture it, fan the flames, and let it illuminate your path to entrepreneurial success. Passion is the fuel that propels you forward, even when the road gets rough.

▷▷▷

TWO

LEAP OF FAITH: OVERCOMING FEARS AND EMBRACING UNCERTAINTY

The path of the solopreneur is seldom a smooth one. It's a terrain marked by challenges, uncertainties, and the ever-present fear of failure. However, within these uncertainties lies the potential for immense growth and extraordinary success. To embark on this journey, one must be willing to take a leap of faith, confronting fears head-on and embracing the unknown with open arms.

Fear is a natural human response to the unfamiliar. It's a primal instinct designed to protect us from potential harm. Yet, when it comes to pursuing our dreams, fear can become a crippling force, holding us back from taking the necessary risks to achieve our goals. The fear of failure, the fear of financial instability, the fear of judgment - these are just a few of the many anxieties that can plague aspiring solopreneurs.

Overcoming these fears requires a shift in perspective. Instead of viewing fear as a roadblock, reframe it as a compass. Fear often points us towards the areas where we need to grow the most. If you're afraid of public speaking, it's a sign that you need to develop your communication skills. If you're afraid of financial instability, it's a call to strengthen your financial literacy and create a solid business plan. Embracing your fears allows you to identify your weaknesses and transform them into strengths.

One of the most effective ways to overcome fear is to face it head-on. Instead of running away from your fears, confront them with courage and determination. This may mean stepping outside your comfort zone, taking calculated risks, and pushing yourself beyond your perceived limits. The more you expose yourself to the things you fear, the less power they will hold over you.

Building resilience is crucial for navigating the uncertainties of solopreneurship. Setbacks and failures are inevitable on this journey. However, it's how you respond to these challenges that will determine your ultimate success. Instead of viewing setbacks as defeats, see them as opportunities for learning and growth. Analyze what went wrong, learn from your mistakes, and use that knowledge to make better decisions in the future.

Embracing uncertainty is a fundamental aspect of the solopreneur's journey. The business landscape is constantly evolving, and there are no guarantees of success. However, it's within this uncertainty that the greatest opportunities often arise. By remaining adaptable and open to new possibilities, you can pivot your strategies, seize unexpected opportunities, and turn challenges into triumphs.

Cultivating a growth mindset is essential for navigating the uncertainties of solopreneurship. Instead of believing that your abilities are fixed, embrace the idea that you can continuously learn and improve. This means seeking out new knowledge, developing new skills, and constantly challenging yourself to grow both personally and professionally.

Building a strong support network can be invaluable for overcoming fears and embracing uncertainty. Surround yourself with positive, supportive people who believe in your vision and encourage your growth. This may include mentors, coaches, fellow solopreneurs, or even friends and family who offer unwavering support.

The solopreneur's journey is not for the faint of heart. It requires a leap of faith, a willingness to face your fears, and an unwavering belief in your own abilities. But for those who dare to embark on this path, the rewards are immeasurable. The freedom to pursue your passions, the satisfaction of creating something meaningful, and the potential for financial independence are just a few of the many benefits of solopreneurship.

Remember, fear is not your enemy. It's a natural human response that can be harnessed for your benefit. By reframing fear as a compass, building resilience, embracing uncertainty, cultivating a growth mindset, and building a strong support network, you can overcome your anxieties and embark on a fulfilling and successful solopreneur journey.

The leap of faith is not a one-time event; it's an ongoing process of self-discovery, growth, and resilience. It's about trusting your instincts, embracing the unknown, and having the courage to pursue your dreams. So, take a deep breath, step off the edge, and soar towards a future filled with limitless possibilities.

ᐅᐅᐅ

The solopreneur's journey is an ever-evolving adventure. Embrace change, adapt to new challenges, and never stop learning and growing. Remember, the path to success is not a straight line, but a winding road filled with unexpected twists and turns. Embrace the journey, for it is in the pursuit of our dreams that we find our true strength and purpose.

❦❦❦

THREE

BLUEPRINT FOR DREAMS: CRAFTING YOUR BUSINESS PLAN

Every grand edifice begins with a blueprint, a meticulously crafted plan that outlines its structure, purpose, and functionality. Similarly, a successful solopreneur venture starts with a comprehensive business plan, a roadmap that guides your journey from ideation to execution. This blueprint for dreams not only serves as a navigational tool but also as a testament to your commitment and vision.

A well-structured business plan is more than just a formality; it's a dynamic document that evolves with your business. It's a living, breathing entity that reflects your aspirations, strategies, and adaptability. At its core, a business plan is a communication tool, designed to articulate your value proposition to potential investors, partners, and clients. It's a testament to your preparedness and a reflection of your entrepreneurial acumen.

The journey of crafting a business plan begins with self-reflection. What are your core values? What problem are you solving? What impact do you want to make? Answering these questions will help you define your mission and vision, the guiding principles that will shape your business decisions.

Next, delve into the market landscape. Who are your target customers? What are their pain points? Who are your competitors? Conducting thorough market research will help you identify your niche, understand your audience, and differentiate yourself from the competition.

Your value proposition is the heart of your business plan. It's a concise statement that articulates the unique benefits your product or service offers to your target market. Your value proposition should be compelling, memorable, and clearly demonstrate how you address your customers' needs better than anyone else.

Once you've defined your value proposition, it's time to develop your marketing and sales strategies. How will you reach your target customers? What channels will you use? What tactics will you employ to convert prospects into loyal clients? A well-thought-out marketing plan will help you create brand awareness, generate leads, and drive sales.

Financial projections are a crucial component of your business plan. They provide a realistic estimate of your revenue, expenses, and profitability over time. While it's impossible to predict the future with absolute certainty, creating financial projections will help you identify potential challenges, set realistic goals, and make informed business decisions.

Your business plan should also outline your operational structure. How will you deliver your product or service? What resources will you need? Who will be responsible for each aspect of your business?

A clear operational plan will ensure smooth execution and minimize the risk of costly mistakes.

Don't forget to include a management and team section. Even as a solopreneur, you may need to collaborate with freelancers, contractors, or advisors. Clearly define the roles and responsibilities of each team member to ensure everyone is working towards a common goal.

A comprehensive business plan also includes a risk assessment and mitigation strategy. Identify potential risks that could derail your business and develop contingency plans to address them. By anticipating challenges and preparing for the unexpected, you can mitigate potential losses and ensure the long-term sustainability of your venture.

Finally, remember that your business plan is not set in stone. It's a living document that should be reviewed and updated regularly. As your business grows and evolves, your plan should adapt to reflect new challenges, opportunities, and learnings.

Crafting a business plan may seem like a daunting task, but it's an essential step towards building a successful solopreneur venture. By taking the time to create a comprehensive blueprint for your dreams, you'll gain clarity, focus, and confidence in your ability to navigate the ever-changing entrepreneurial landscape. Your business plan is not just a document; it's a testament to your vision, your commitment, and your potential for success.

ᚦᚦᚦ

Embrace the unknown, for it is in the realm of uncertainty that true growth occurs. Take that leap of faith, for it is in the face of fear that we discover our greatest strengths. Remember, the only limits that exist are the ones we impose upon ourselves.

❥❥❥

FOUR

SOLO, BUT NOT ALONE: BUILDING A SUPPORT NETWORK

The life of a solopreneur can be exhilarating, filled with freedom, creativity, and the thrill of building something from the ground up. Yet, it's also a path that can feel isolating at times. The absence of colleagues, the lack of a traditional team structure, and the weight of decision-making can leave solopreneurs feeling like lone wolves in the vast wilderness of entrepreneurship.

However, the reality is that solopreneurs are far from alone. Building a strong support network is crucial for navigating the challenges, celebrating the triumphs, and achieving long-term success. A support network acts as a lifeline, providing guidance, encouragement, and a sense of community when the going gets tough. It's a source of inspiration, accountability, and a sounding board for ideas.

One of the most valuable components of a support network is mentorship. A mentor is a seasoned professional who has walked the path before you and can offer invaluable insights, advice, and guidance. They can help you avoid common pitfalls, navigate complex challenges, and accelerate your growth. Seek out mentors who share your values, understand your industry, and have a track record of success. Their wisdom and experience can be a game-changer for your solopreneur journey.

Peer-to-peer connections are equally important. Connecting with other solopreneurs in your industry or niche can provide a sense of camaraderie, a space for sharing experiences, and a platform for collaboration. Join online forums, attend industry events, or participate in co-working spaces to connect with like-minded individuals who understand the unique challenges and rewards of solopreneurship. These connections can lead to valuable partnerships, collaborations, and friendships that enrich your entrepreneurial journey.

Don't underestimate the power of your personal network. Friends, family, and loved ones can offer unwavering support, encouragement, and a listening ear when you need it most. Share your dreams, challenges, and successes with them. Their belief in you can be a powerful motivator and a source of strength when faced with setbacks.

In addition to personal connections, professional networks can also play a vital role in your support system. Join industry associations, attend networking events, and connect with potential clients, partners, and collaborators. These connections can open doors to new opportunities, provide valuable feedback, and expand your reach in the market.

Building a support network is not a one-time event; it's an ongoing process that requires effort and intention. Nurture your relationships, reciprocate support, and be willing to give as much as you receive. Actively seek out new connections, attend events, and engage in online communities. The more you invest in building your support network, the more you'll reap the benefits.

A strong support network can provide a multitude of benefits for solopreneurs. It can help you stay motivated, focused, and accountable. It can offer a sounding board for ideas, a source of inspiration, and a safe space for vulnerability. It can connect you with valuable resources, opportunities, and collaborations. And most importantly, it can remind you that you're not alone on this journey.

Remember, building a support network is not a sign of weakness; it's a sign of strength. It takes courage to admit that you need help, to reach out to others, and to build meaningful connections. But by investing in your support network, you're investing in your own success. You're creating a foundation of support, encouragement, and community that will empower you to overcome challenges, achieve your goals, and thrive as a solopreneur.

So, don't go it alone. Build a support network that empowers, inspires, and uplifts you. Surround yourself with people who believe in your vision, challenge you to grow, and celebrate your successes. Together, you can navigate the exciting and rewarding path of solopreneurship with confidence, resilience, and joy.

ᗡᗡᗡ

Your business plan is not just a document; it's a living, breathing testament to your dreams. Craft it with care, nurture it with passion, and let it guide you towards your entrepreneurial destiny. A well-crafted plan is a compass that keeps you on course, even when the storms of doubt rage around you.

⊳⊳⊳

FIVE

Mastering the Juggle: Balancing Work and Life

The solopreneur's journey is often a thrilling tightrope walk, balancing the demands of a burgeoning business with the necessities and joys of personal life. This delicate dance requires not just skill and focus, but a well-honed strategy for maintaining equilibrium. The elusive work-life balance, a holy grail for many, is an attainable reality for solopreneurs who embrace conscious choices and proactive measures.

At the heart of this balancing act lies the art of boundary setting. Without the traditional confines of a 9-to-5 job, solopreneurs must define their own parameters. This involves creating a clear distinction between work hours and personal time, establishing a dedicated workspace, and communicating these boundaries to clients, family, and friends. It's about respecting your own time and energy, and ensuring that your work doesn't bleed into every aspect of your life.

Time management is another crucial element in mastering the

juggle. As the sole proprietor of your business, you're responsible for every aspect of its operation. This can easily lead to overwhelm and burnout if not managed effectively. Prioritizing tasks, delegating where possible, and utilizing time management tools can help you maximize productivity and minimize stress. It's about working smarter, not harder, and making the most of your valuable time.

One of the most common pitfalls for solopreneurs is the tendency to overwork. The passion and drive that fuel entrepreneurship can easily lead to long hours, neglected personal needs, and ultimately, burnout. It's essential to recognize the signs of burnout and take proactive measures to prevent it. This might involve setting strict work hours, scheduling regular breaks, taking vacations, and engaging in activities that recharge your batteries. Remember, a well-rested and rejuvenated solopreneur is a more productive and creative one.

The pursuit of work-life balance isn't just about managing time; it's also about managing energy. Different tasks require different levels of mental and physical energy. By understanding your own energy cycles, you can schedule demanding tasks for when you're most alert and creative, and reserve less taxing activities for times when your energy is lower. This approach not only optimizes productivity but also prevents burnout.

Technology, while a powerful tool for solopreneurs, can also be a double-edged sword. The constant connectivity and accessibility afforded by technology can blur the lines between work and personal life, making it difficult to disconnect and recharge. Setting boundaries for technology use, such as turning off notifications after work hours or designating tech-free zones, can help you reclaim your personal time and maintain a healthy balance.

Self-care is not a luxury for solopreneurs; it's a necessity. Taking care of your physical, mental, and emotional well-being is essential for maintaining productivity, creativity, and overall happiness. This might involve regular exercise, healthy eating, mindfulness practices, or simply taking time to relax and recharge. Remember, you can't pour from an empty cup.

Building a support system is crucial for maintaining work-life balance. Surround yourself with people who understand the unique challenges of solopreneurship and can offer support, encouragement, and advice. This might include mentors, fellow solopreneurs, friends, family, or even a therapist. Having people to lean on can make a world of difference when the going gets tough.

It's important to remember that work-life balance is not a static state; it's an ongoing process that requires constant adjustment and adaptation. As your business grows and evolves, your priorities and needs will also change. Be willing to reassess your boundaries, redefine your goals, and experiment with different strategies to find what works best for you.

The pursuit of work-life balance is a personal journey. There's no one-size-fits-all solution. What works for one solopreneur may not work for another. The key is to be intentional, self-aware, and willing to experiment. By prioritizing your well-being, setting boundaries, managing your time and energy effectively, and building a strong support system, you can create a fulfilling and sustainable solopreneur lifestyle that allows you to thrive both personally and professionally.

ᐁᐁᐁ

Solo, but never alone. The solopreneur's journey is enriched by a tapestry of connections, mentorships, and collaborations. Build your tribe, for it is in the company of like-minded individuals that we find strength, support, and inspiration. Remember, the collective wisdom of a community can elevate your business to new heights.

SIX

Money Matters: Financial Planning for Solopreneurs

Money matters. It's a simple truth that echoes through the corridors of every entrepreneurial venture, but it holds particular significance for solopreneurs. As the sole proprietor of your business, you are not just the visionary and the executor, but also the financial steward. Financial planning is not merely a task; it's a mindset, a continuous process that requires diligence, discipline, and a keen understanding of your business's financial health.

At the outset, it's imperative to establish a clear separation between your personal and business finances. This involves opening a separate bank account for your business, obtaining a business credit card, and meticulously tracking all income and expenses. This segregation not only simplifies accounting but also provides a clear picture of your business's financial performance, enabling you to make informed decisions.

Budgeting is the cornerstone of financial planning. It's a roadmap that outlines your income, expenses, and savings goals. Start by forecasting your revenue based on your sales projections and pricing strategy. Then, meticulously track your expenses, categorizing them into fixed costs (rent, utilities, etc.) and variable costs (marketing, inventory, etc.). Your budget should also include a contingency fund for unexpected expenses and a savings plan for taxes and future investments.

Cash flow management is another critical aspect of financial planning. It's not just about how much money you make, but also about when you receive it and when you need to pay your bills. A cash flow statement tracks the inflow and outflow of cash, providing a real-time view of your financial health. By monitoring your cash flow, you can identify potential shortfalls, adjust your spending, and ensure that you always have enough funds to meet your obligations.

Pricing your products or services is a delicate balancing act. You need to charge enough to cover your costs, make a profit, and remain competitive in the market. Conduct thorough market research to understand your customers' willingness to pay and your competitors' pricing strategies. Consider offering different pricing tiers or packages to cater to different customer segments. Regularly review your pricing strategy to ensure it aligns with your financial goals and market conditions.

Taxes are an inevitable part of doing business. As a solopreneur, you're responsible for understanding and complying with tax regulations. This includes registering your business, obtaining the necessary permits and licenses, and filing your tax returns on time. Consider consulting a tax professional to ensure you're taking advantage of all available deductions and credits.

Investing in your business is essential for growth. This could involve upgrading your equipment, expanding your marketing efforts, or hiring additional help. However, it's crucial to invest wisely and avoid overspending. Create a long-term investment plan that aligns with your business goals and budget. Consider seeking advice from financial advisors or mentors who can help you make informed investment decisions.

Managing debt is a reality for many solopreneurs. Whether it's a business loan, a credit card balance, or personal debt, it's important to have a plan for managing and reducing your debt. Prioritize high-interest debt and explore debt consolidation options if necessary. Make timely payments and avoid accumulating unnecessary debt that could jeopardize your financial stability.

Financial planning for solopreneurs is not a one-time event; it's an ongoing process that requires constant vigilance and adaptation. Regularly review your budget, cash flow, and financial goals. Stay informed about changes in tax regulations and market trends. Seek advice from financial professionals when needed. By staying on top of your finances, you can mitigate risks, capitalize on opportunities, and build a financially sustainable business.

Remember, money matters are not just about numbers; they're about your dreams, your goals, and your future. By taking a proactive and strategic approach to financial planning, you can empower yourself to make informed decisions, achieve financial independence, and build a thriving solopreneur venture that not only sustains you but also contributes to your community and the world.

ppp

Mastering the juggle between work and life is an art form. Set boundaries, prioritize self-care, and embrace the flexibility that solopreneurship offers. Remember, a balanced life is a fulfilling life, and a happy solopreneur is a successful solopreneur.

▷▷▷

SEVEN

Marketing Mojo: Attracting and Engaging Clients

Attracting and engaging clients is the lifeblood of any solopreneur venture. It's the magic that transforms your passion and expertise into a thriving business. However, in a world saturated with marketing messages, standing out from the crowd and capturing the attention of your ideal clients requires a unique blend of creativity, strategy, and authenticity.

At the heart of successful marketing lies a deep understanding of your target audience. Who are they? What are their pain points? What motivates them? What channels do they frequent? By delving into the minds and hearts of your ideal clients, you can tailor your messaging, choose the right platforms, and create content that resonates with them on a personal level.

Crafting a compelling brand identity is essential for attracting clients. Your brand is more than just a logo or a tagline; it's the essence of your business, the promise you make to your customers. It's what sets you apart from the competition and makes you memorable. Your brand should reflect your values, your personality, and the unique benefits you offer. It should be consistent across all touchpoints, from your website and social media profiles to your client interactions and marketing materials.

Content marketing is a powerful tool for engaging clients. By creating valuable, informative, and entertaining content that addresses your audience's needs and interests, you can establish yourself as an authority in your field, build trust, and attract potential clients. This content can take many forms, such as blog posts, articles, videos, podcasts, social media posts, or even ebooks and webinars. The key is to provide value first and foremost, and to promote your products or services subtly and authentically.

Social media has revolutionized the way businesses connect with their audience. By leveraging the power of social media platforms, you can reach a vast audience, build relationships, and drive traffic to your website. Choose the platforms where your target audience is most active and create engaging content that sparks conversations and encourages sharing. Don't just broadcast your message; interact with your followers, respond to comments, and participate in relevant discussions.

Email marketing remains a highly effective tool for nurturing leads and converting them into clients. By building an email list of interested prospects, you can send them targeted messages that educate, inform, and entice them to take action. Offer valuable incentives, such as free resources or exclusive discounts, to encourage people to sign up for your list. Then, send regular emails that provide value, build relationships, and subtly promote your products or services.

Networking is a vital component of client acquisition for solopreneurs. Attend industry events, join online communities, and connect with potential clients and collaborators. Don't be afraid to put yourself out there, share your expertise, and build genuine relationships. Networking can lead to valuable referrals, partnerships, and new business opportunities.

Building strong client relationships is essential for long-term success. Go above and beyond to exceed your clients' expectations, deliver exceptional service, and communicate proactively. Offer personalized attention, solicit feedback, and address any concerns promptly. By nurturing your client relationships, you can turn them into loyal advocates who will not only continue to do business with you but also refer you to others.

In the ever-evolving world of marketing, it's important to stay ahead of the curve. Experiment with new platforms, try different strategies, and track your results. Don't be afraid to take risks and try something new. The most successful solopreneurs are those who are willing to adapt, innovate, and constantly refine their marketing approach.

Marketing is not just about attracting clients; it's about building relationships, fostering trust, and creating a loyal community of supporters. By understanding your audience, crafting a compelling brand, creating valuable content, leveraging social media, utilizing email marketing, networking effectively, and building strong client relationships, you can create a marketing mojo that will not only attract and engage clients but also propel your solopreneur venture to new heights.

ৡৡৡ

Money matters, but it's not the sole measure of success. Financial planning is about more than just numbers; it's about creating a sustainable future for your business and your dreams. Take charge of your finances, make informed decisions, and invest in your growth, for it is through financial stability that you can truly thrive as a solopreneur.

❥❥❥

EIGHT

TECH TOOLKIT: ESSENTIAL TOOLS FOR DIGITAL SUCCESS

In the digital age, technology is the solopreneur's most trusted companion. It's a toolbox overflowing with possibilities, empowering you to streamline operations, connect with clients, amplify your message, and achieve unprecedented levels of productivity. But with a vast array of tools available, it can be overwhelming to determine which ones are truly essential for your solopreneur journey.

At the foundation of your tech toolkit lies a robust and reliable computer system. Whether you prefer a laptop for its portability or a desktop for its power, investing in a high-performance machine will pay dividends in terms of speed, efficiency, and overall productivity. A fast processor, ample storage, and sufficient RAM will ensure that your computer can handle demanding tasks, from graphic design and video editing to complex data analysis and software development.

Cloud storage is a game-changer for solopreneurs. It allows you to store, access, and share your files from anywhere, on any device. This not only provides a convenient backup solution but also enables seamless collaboration with clients and team members. Popular cloud storage providers like Dropbox, Google Drive, and OneDrive offer various plans to suit different needs and budgets.

A website is your virtual storefront, your online home. It's where potential clients discover your brand, learn about your products or services, and decide whether to engage with you. A well-designed website should be visually appealing, easy to navigate, and optimized for mobile devices. Consider using a website builder like Wix, Squarespace, or WordPress to create a professional-looking website without needing to code.

Email marketing is a cornerstone of digital marketing for solopreneurs. It allows you to build relationships with potential clients, nurture leads, and drive sales. Email marketing platforms like Mailchimp, ConvertKit, and ActiveCampaign offer a range of features, including customizable templates, automation tools, and analytics to track your campaign performance.

Social media is a powerful tool for connecting with your target audience, building brand awareness, and driving traffic to your website. Choose the platforms where your ideal clients are most active and create engaging content that sparks conversations and encourages sharing. Tools like Hootsuite and Buffer can help you schedule posts, manage multiple accounts, and track your social media performance.

Project management tools are essential for keeping track of tasks, deadlines, and progress. Platforms like Asana, Trello, and Monday.com offer a visual way to organize your projects, assign tasks to team members, and track progress in real time. This helps you stay organized, prioritize your work, and ensure that projects are completed on time and within budget.

Communication tools are vital for staying connected with clients, team members, and collaborators. Video conferencing platforms like Zoom, Skype, and Google Meet enable face-to-face communication, while messaging apps like Slack and Microsoft Teams facilitate real-time collaboration. Choose the tools that best suit your communication style and workflow.

Accounting software is a must-have for managing your finances. Platforms like QuickBooks, Xero, and FreshBooks automate invoicing, expense tracking, and financial reporting, saving you time and ensuring accuracy. They also integrate with other tools, such as payment processors and bank accounts, for seamless financial management.

Cybersecurity is a top priority for any business operating online. Protect your data and your clients' information by investing in reliable antivirus software, a firewall, and a password manager. Educate yourself and your team about cybersecurity best practices to prevent data breaches and other cyber threats.

The tech toolkit for solopreneurs is constantly evolving. New tools and technologies emerge regularly, offering new possibilities and efficiencies. Stay informed about the latest trends, experiment with different tools, and choose the ones that best suit your needs and budget. By leveraging the power of technology, you can streamline your operations, enhance your productivity, and achieve digital success as a solopreneur.

▷▷▷

Marketing is the magic that connects your passion with your audience. Craft a compelling brand story, engage with your community, and let your authentic voice shine through. Remember, the most successful marketing is not about selling; it's about building relationships and fostering trust.

❦❦❦

NINE

CLIENT WHISPERER: BUILDING STRONG RELATIONSHIPS

In the world of solopreneurship, where every client interaction is a potential turning point, the ability to build strong relationships is not just an advantage, but a necessity. It's about transcending the transactional nature of business and forging genuine connections that foster trust, loyalty, and mutual respect. A solopreneur who masters the art of client whispering can unlock a wealth of opportunities, referrals, and long-term success.

At its core, building strong client relationships is about understanding and anticipating their needs. It's about listening attentively, asking insightful questions, and demonstrating a genuine interest in their goals and challenges. It's about putting yourself in their shoes and seeing the world from their perspective. This empathy allows you to tailor your solutions, communication style, and overall approach to resonate with each client on a personal level.

Effective communication is the cornerstone of any strong

relationship. It's not just about exchanging information; it's about fostering understanding, building rapport, and creating a sense of partnership. Be clear, concise, and transparent in your communication. Set expectations upfront, provide regular updates, and be responsive to inquiries and concerns. Use language that is respectful, professional, and tailored to your client's communication style. Whether it's a formal email or a casual conversation, every interaction is an opportunity to strengthen the bond with your client.

Building trust is a gradual process that requires consistency, reliability, and integrity. Deliver on your promises, meet deadlines, and exceed expectations whenever possible. Be transparent about your process, communicate any challenges or setbacks proactively, and offer solutions. By consistently demonstrating your commitment to their success, you can earn your client's trust and loyalty.

Going above and beyond is a hallmark of exceptional client service. It's about anticipating your client's needs before they even realize them, offering proactive solutions, and adding value at every turn. This could involve providing additional resources, offering personalized recommendations, or simply checking in to see how they're doing. By consistently exceeding expectations, you can create a memorable client experience that sets you apart from the competition.

Building strong client relationships is not just about providing excellent service; it's also about fostering a genuine connection. Take the time to get to know your clients on a personal level. Learn about their interests, their families, their aspirations. Share your own stories and experiences. By building rapport and creating a sense of shared humanity, you can transform a transactional relationship into a meaningful connection.

In the digital age, where much of our communication happens online, it's important to find ways to humanize your interactions. Use video calls to create a sense of face-to-face connection, send personalized thank-you notes, or even surprise your clients with small gifts or tokens of appreciation. These small gestures can go a long way in building rapport and strengthening the relationship.

Don't be afraid to ask for feedback. Regularly solicit feedback from your clients to gauge their satisfaction, identify areas for improvement, and demonstrate your commitment to their success. Use this feedback constructively to refine your approach, enhance your services, and exceed their expectations.

Remember, building strong client relationships is an ongoing process that requires continuous effort and dedication. It's not just about closing deals; it's about building lasting partnerships. By investing in your client relationships, you're investing in the long-term success and sustainability of your solopreneur venture. The relationships you build today can open doors to new opportunities, referrals, and collaborations in the future.

The art of client whispering is a skill that can be learned and honed over time. It requires empathy, communication skills, trustworthiness, and a genuine desire to help your clients succeed. By mastering this art, you can transform your clients into loyal advocates, your business into a thriving enterprise, and your solopreneur journey into a fulfilling and rewarding experience.

ᛈᛈᛈ

Technology is your ally, not your master. Embrace the tools that empower you, automate the mundane, and unleash your creative potential. Remember, technology is a means to an end, not the end itself. Use it wisely, and it will amplify your impact.

❦❦❦

TEN

RESILIENCE ROADMAP: BOUNCING BACK FROM SETBACKS

The solopreneur's journey is not always a smooth ascent. It's a winding path marked by unexpected detours, unforeseen challenges, and occasional setbacks. These setbacks can range from minor inconveniences to major crises, testing your resolve, resilience, and ability to adapt. However, setbacks are not roadblocks; they are stepping stones on the path to success. The ability to bounce back from setbacks is not just a desirable trait; it's a non-negotiable skill for any solopreneur who aspires to thrive in the ever-changing entrepreneurial landscape.

Resilience is the bedrock upon which solopreneurs build their empires. It's the inner strength that allows you to weather storms, overcome obstacles, and emerge stronger than ever. It's the ability to adapt to changing circumstances, learn from mistakes, and maintain a positive outlook even in the face of adversity. Resilience is not a fixed trait; it's a muscle that can be developed and strengthened over time.

One of the keys to building resilience is to cultivate a growth mindset. Instead of viewing setbacks as failures, see them as opportunities for learning and growth. Analyze what went wrong, identify the lessons learned, and use that knowledge to make better decisions in the future. Embrace the idea that setbacks are not the end of the road but rather detours that can lead to new and unexpected paths.

Developing a strong support system is crucial for bouncing back from setbacks. Surround yourself with positive, supportive people who believe in your vision and encourage your growth. This might include mentors, coaches, fellow solopreneurs, friends, family, or even a therapist. Having people to lean on during challenging times can provide invaluable emotional support, practical advice, and a fresh perspective.

Self-care is an essential component of resilience. When faced with setbacks, it's easy to neglect your own well-being. However, taking care of your physical, mental, and emotional health is crucial for maintaining your energy, focus, and resilience. This might involve regular exercise, healthy eating, mindfulness practices, or simply taking time to relax and recharge. Remember, a healthy and balanced solopreneur is better equipped to handle challenges and bounce back from setbacks.

Another key to resilience is the ability to adapt to change. The entrepreneurial landscape is constantly evolving, and what worked yesterday may not work tomorrow. Be willing to pivot your strategies, embrace new technologies, and adapt to changing market conditions. Flexibility and adaptability are essential for navigating the uncertainties of solopreneurship and bouncing back from setbacks.

Maintaining a positive outlook is crucial for overcoming challenges. When faced with setbacks, it's easy to fall into a spiral of negativity and self-doubt. However, cultivating a positive mindset can help you reframe challenges as opportunities, maintain motivation, and find creative solutions. Practice gratitude, celebrate small wins, and focus on the bigger picture. A positive attitude can be a powerful tool for overcoming adversity and achieving success.

Learning from mistakes is a hallmark of resilient solopreneurs. Don't be afraid to fail; embrace it as a learning experience. Analyze what went wrong, identify the lessons learned, and use that knowledge to make better decisions in the future. Remember, every successful entrepreneur has experienced setbacks along the way. It's how you respond to those setbacks that will determine your ultimate success.

Developing coping mechanisms is essential for dealing with the stress and challenges of solopreneurship. Find healthy ways to manage stress, such as exercise, meditation, or spending time in nature. Build a routine that prioritizes your well-being and allows you to recharge your batteries. By taking care of yourself, you'll be better equipped to handle the ups and downs of the entrepreneurial journey.

Bouncing back from setbacks is not about denying or suppressing negative emotions; it's about acknowledging them, processing them, and then moving forward. Allow yourself to feel the disappointment, frustration, or anger that comes with setbacks. But don't dwell on those emotions. Instead, channel them into positive action. Use your setbacks as fuel to ignite your passion, rekindle your motivation, and propel you towards your goals.

Remember, resilience is not a destination; it's a journey. It's a continuous process of learning, adapting, and growing. By cultivating a growth mindset, building a strong support system, prioritizing self-care, embracing change, maintaining a positive outlook, learning from mistakes, and developing coping mechanisms, you can build the resilience you need to overcome any setback and achieve lasting success as a solopreneur.

ϸϸϸ

Your clients are not just customers; they are partners in your journey. Listen to their needs, exceed their expectations, and build relationships that last a lifetime. Remember, a loyal client is worth more than a thousand fleeting transactions.

ᗵᗵᗵ

ELEVEN

GROWTH MINDSET: CULTIVATING A THIRST FOR LEARNING

The solopreneur's journey is not a sprint, but a marathon. It's a continuous process of growth, evolution, and adaptation. To thrive in this dynamic landscape, one must cultivate a growth mindset, an insatiable thirst for learning that fuels innovation, propels personal development, and ensures long-term success. This mindset is not merely about acquiring knowledge; it's about embracing challenges, celebrating failures as stepping stones, and constantly seeking opportunities for improvement.

At its core, a growth mindset is a belief in one's own ability to learn and grow. It's a rejection of the notion that intelligence and talent are fixed traits, and an embrace of the idea that with effort, dedication, and perseverance, we can expand our capabilities and achieve our goals. This mindset is a powerful catalyst for personal and professional development, as it empowers us to step outside our comfort zones, take risks, and embrace challenges as opportunities for growth.

In the context of solopreneurship, a growth mindset is essential for navigating the ever-changing entrepreneurial landscape. The business world is constantly evolving, with new technologies, trends, and challenges emerging at a rapid pace. A solopreneur with a growth mindset embraces these changes as opportunities to learn, adapt, and innovate. They view challenges not as roadblocks, but as stepping stones on the path to success.

Cultivating a growth mindset requires a shift in perspective. It's about reframing failure as a learning experience, embracing feedback as a gift, and viewing challenges as opportunities for growth. Instead of fearing mistakes, solopreneurs with a growth mindset see them as valuable lessons that pave the way for future success. They understand that failure is not the opposite of success, but rather a stepping stone on the path to achieving it.

One of the most effective ways to cultivate a growth mindset is to embrace a lifelong learning approach. This means constantly seeking out new knowledge, skills, and experiences. Read books, attend workshops, take online courses, listen to podcasts, and engage with thought leaders in your industry. The more you expose yourself to new ideas and perspectives, the more you'll expand your knowledge base, enhance your skills, and fuel your creativity.

Mentorship can play a crucial role in developing a growth mindset. A mentor is a trusted advisor who can offer guidance, support, and encouragement as you navigate your entrepreneurial journey. They can share their own experiences, provide valuable feedback, and challenge you to think outside the box. Seek out mentors who have a growth mindset themselves and who are passionate about helping others succeed.

Networking with other entrepreneurs can also foster a growth mindset. Surround yourself with individuals who are passionate about learning, who embrace challenges, and who are constantly striving to improve. By engaging in conversations, sharing ideas, and collaborating on projects, you can learn from their experiences, gain new perspectives, and expand your own knowledge base.

Another key to cultivating a growth mindset is to practice self-reflection. Regularly assess your strengths, weaknesses, and areas for improvement. Set goals, track your progress, and celebrate your achievements. By reflecting on your journey, you can identify patterns, learn from your mistakes, and make adjustments as needed.

Embracing feedback is essential for growth. Seek feedback from mentors, colleagues, clients, and even competitors. Use this feedback constructively to identify areas where you can improve, refine your strategies, and enhance your performance. Remember, feedback is not a personal attack; it's a valuable tool for growth and development.

A growth mindset is not just about acquiring knowledge and skills; it's also about developing resilience, perseverance, and a positive attitude. Embrace challenges as opportunities for growth, view setbacks as learning experiences, and maintain a positive outlook even in the face of adversity. By cultivating a growth mindset, you can unlock your full potential, achieve your goals, and create a fulfilling and successful solopreneur journey.

Setbacks are not roadblocks; they are detours on the path to success. Embrace them as learning opportunities, rise above challenges, and emerge stronger than ever. Remember, resilience is the cornerstone of solopreneurship, and it is in the face of adversity that we truly discover our strength.

ppp

TWELVE

THE SOLOPRENEUR'S BRAND: CREATING YOUR UNIQUE IDENTITY

In the vast and bustling marketplace of ideas, products, and services, a solopreneur's brand serves as their North Star, guiding them through the competitive landscape and illuminating their path to success. It's more than just a logo or a catchy tagline; it's the essence of who you are as an entrepreneur, the values you embody, the promises you make, and the experiences you deliver. It's the unique identity that sets you apart from the crowd, attracts your ideal clients, and builds a loyal following.

Creating a strong brand identity is not a luxury for solopreneurs; it's a necessity. In a world where consumers are bombarded with choices, a well-defined brand can make all the difference between being noticed and being overlooked. It's the foundation upon which you build trust, credibility, and loyalty. It's the magnet that attracts your ideal clients and repels those who aren't a good fit.

The journey of crafting your solopreneur brand begins with self-reflection. What are your core values? What are your passions? What unique skills and experiences do you bring to the table? What problems do you solve for your clients? What impact do you want to make on the world? Answering these questions will help you define your brand's purpose, its reason for being.

Your brand story is the narrative that connects your purpose with your audience. It's the story of how you came to be, the challenges you overcame, the lessons you learned, and the passions that drive you. It's the human element that makes your brand relatable, authentic, and memorable. Share your story through your website, social media, blog posts, or even in conversations with clients. Let your audience connect with you on a personal level and see the human behind the brand.

Your visual identity is the face of your brand. It's the first impression you make on potential clients, and it plays a crucial role in shaping their perception of your business. Your logo, color palette, typography, and overall design aesthetic should reflect your brand's personality, values, and target audience. Consistency is key. Ensure that your visual identity is cohesive across all touchpoints, from your website and social media profiles to your business cards and marketing materials.

Your brand voice is the tone and style of your communication. It's how you express your brand's personality and connect with your audience. Whether it's witty, informative, inspirational, or quirky, your brand voice should be consistent across all channels, from your website copy and social media posts to your email newsletters and client interactions. A well-defined brand voice helps you build a strong connection with your audience and establish a distinct identity in the marketplace.

Your brand promise is the commitment you make to your clients. It's the value you offer, the problems you solve, and the results you deliver. Your brand promise should be clear, concise, and compelling. It should be something that your clients can believe in and rely on. Delivering on your brand promise is essential for building trust and loyalty.

Building a strong brand takes time, effort, and consistency. It's an ongoing process that requires constant attention and refinement. Be authentic, be consistent, and be true to your values. Listen to your audience, engage with them, and build relationships. Your brand is not just a marketing tool; it's a reflection of who you are as a solopreneur. It's your legacy, your contribution to the world.

In the digital age, your online presence is an extension of your brand. Your website, social media profiles, and online content should all reflect your brand's identity and values. Create a cohesive online presence that showcases your expertise, highlights your unique value proposition, and engages your audience. Use high-quality visuals, compelling copy, and a consistent brand voice to create a memorable online experience.

Don't be afraid to let your personality shine through your brand. People connect with people, not with faceless corporations. Share your passions, your quirks, and your unique perspective. Be authentic, be genuine, and be yourself. Your authenticity will resonate with your audience and help you build a loyal following.

Remember, your brand is not just about what you say; it's about what you do. Your actions, your interactions, and your commitment to delivering on your promises all contribute to your brand's reputation. Strive to provide exceptional service, exceed expectations, and go above and beyond for your clients. Your reputation is your most valuable asset, and it's built one interaction at a time.

Creating your unique brand identity is a journey of self-discovery, creativity, and strategic thinking. It's about understanding your values, defining your purpose, crafting a compelling story, and consistently delivering on your promises. By investing in your brand, you're investing in your future. You're creating a legacy that will not only benefit your business but also leave a lasting impact on the world.

ϸϸϸ

A growth mindset is the solopreneur's superpower. Embrace lifelong learning, challenge your assumptions, and seek out new experiences. Remember, the only limit to your growth is the limit of your imagination.

❦❦❦

THIRTEEN

PRODUCTIVITY POWER-UPS: OPTIMIZING YOUR WORKFLOW

The solopreneur's path is paved with a multitude of tasks, responsibilities, and aspirations. To navigate this dynamic landscape and achieve optimal results, one must harness the power of productivity. It's about working smarter, not harder, and finding the right tools, techniques, and mindset to optimize your workflow, maximize your time, and achieve your goals.

A crucial first step in boosting productivity is gaining clarity on your goals and priorities. What are you trying to achieve? What tasks are most important for moving the needle in your business? By identifying your top priorities, you can focus your energy and resources on the activities that truly matter, rather than getting bogged down in less impactful tasks. This requires a conscious effort to evaluate your to-do list regularly and ruthlessly prioritize the most important items.

Time management is the cornerstone of productivity. It's about making the most of your most valuable resource: your time. This involves setting realistic deadlines, breaking down large tasks into smaller, more manageable chunks, and allocating specific time slots for different activities. Consider using time management techniques like the Pomodoro Technique, which involves working in focused bursts followed by short breaks, to maximize focus and prevent burnout.

One of the most effective ways to optimize your workflow is to automate repetitive tasks. There are a multitude of tools available that can automate everything from email marketing and social media scheduling to invoicing and expense tracking. By automating these tasks, you free up valuable time and mental energy to focus on more strategic and creative aspects of your business.

The right tools can be a game-changer for productivity. Invest in software and applications that streamline your workflow, automate tasks, and enhance collaboration. Project management tools, communication platforms, accounting software, and customer relationship management (CRM) systems are just a few examples of tools that can significantly boost your productivity.

Creating a dedicated workspace is essential for maintaining focus and minimizing distractions. Whether it's a home office, a co-working space, or a quiet corner in a cafe, having a designated area where you can concentrate on your work can significantly improve your productivity. Ensure your workspace is well-lit, comfortable, and free from distractions. Personalize it with items that inspire and motivate you.

Taking breaks is not a sign of laziness; it's a strategic move to recharge your batteries and maintain peak performance. Studies have shown that short breaks throughout the day can improve focus, creativity, and overall productivity. Step away from your desk, go for a walk, listen to music, or engage in a quick meditation session. These short breaks can help you clear your head, reduce stress, and return to your work with renewed energy and focus.

Delegation is a powerful productivity tool for solopreneurs. While it may seem counterintuitive to outsource tasks when you're running a one-person business, delegating non-essential tasks can free up your time to focus on your core competencies and high-impact activities. Consider hiring freelancers or virtual assistants to handle tasks like social media management, bookkeeping, or administrative tasks.

Maintaining a healthy work-life balance is crucial for long-term productivity and well-being. Solopreneurs often struggle with setting boundaries between work and personal life, leading to burnout and decreased productivity. Make time for activities that you enjoy, spend time with loved ones, and prioritize your physical and mental health. A well-rested and rejuvenated mind is a more productive one.

Continuous learning is essential for staying ahead of the curve in the fast-paced entrepreneurial world. Invest in your professional development by attending workshops, conferences, or online courses. Read industry publications, listen to podcasts, and network with other entrepreneurs. The more you learn, the more you'll grow, and the more effective you'll become as a solopreneur.

The pursuit of productivity is an ongoing journey. It's about experimenting with different tools, techniques, and strategies to find what works best for you. It's about constantly evaluating your workflow, identifying areas for improvement, and making adjustments as needed. By prioritizing your goals, managing your time effectively, automating tasks, utilizing the right tools, creating a dedicated workspace, taking breaks, delegating, maintaining a healthy work-life balance, and embracing continuous learning, you can unlock your full potential and achieve extraordinary results as a solopreneur.

ᐳᐳᐳ

Your brand is your legacy, your unique mark on the world. Craft it with intention, infuse it with your personality, and let it shine brightly. Remember, a strong brand is not just about recognition; it's about creating a lasting impact.

♡♡♡

FOURTEEN

LEGAL LANDSCAPE: UNDERSTANDING CONTRACTS AND COMPLIANCE

Embarking on the solopreneur journey is a thrilling adventure, filled with endless possibilities and the promise of autonomy. However, amidst the excitement, it's crucial not to overlook the legal landscape that underpins every business venture. Understanding contracts and compliance is not just a matter of legality; it's a safeguard for your business, a shield that protects your interests, and a foundation for building trust with clients and partners.

Contracts are the bedrock of any business relationship. They are legally binding agreements that outline the rights, responsibilities, and expectations of each party involved. A well-drafted contract can prevent misunderstandings, mitigate risks, and provide a clear path for dispute resolution. Whether it's a simple service agreement or a complex partnership agreement, every contract should be carefully crafted to protect your interests and ensure clarity and transparency.

When entering into a contract, it's essential to understand the key terms and conditions. This includes the scope of work, payment terms, deadlines, termination clauses, and dispute resolution mechanisms. Don't hesitate to seek legal advice if you're unsure about any aspect of the contract. It's always better to be safe than sorry, and a lawyer can help you navigate the complexities of contract law and ensure that your interests are protected.

Compliance is another critical aspect of the legal landscape. As a solopreneur, you're responsible for adhering to various laws and regulations that govern your industry and business operations. This includes obtaining the necessary licenses and permits, paying taxes, complying with labor laws, and protecting consumer data. Ignoring compliance requirements can lead to hefty fines, legal disputes, and damage to your reputation.

It's important to stay informed about the specific regulations that apply to your business. This might involve researching industry-specific laws, consulting with legal professionals, and attending workshops or webinars on legal compliance. Keep abreast of any changes in regulations and ensure that your business practices are always up-to-date.

Intellectual property (IP) protection is another crucial aspect of the legal landscape. Your ideas, inventions, designs, and creative works are valuable assets that need to be protected. This includes trademarks, copyrights, patents, and trade secrets. By registering your intellectual property, you can prevent others from using it without your permission and ensure that you receive proper recognition and compensation for your creations.

Privacy and data protection are paramount in today's digital age. As a solopreneur, you're likely collecting and storing sensitive client information, such as names, addresses, email addresses, and payment details. It's your responsibility to protect this data from unauthorized access, disclosure, or misuse. This involves implementing robust security measures, such as encryption, firewalls, and regular backups. It also means being transparent with your clients about how you collect, use, and store their data.

Navigating the legal landscape can be daunting, especially for solopreneurs who may not have a legal background. However, it's not something to be taken lightly. By understanding contracts, complying with regulations, protecting your intellectual property, and prioritizing privacy and data protection, you can create a solid legal foundation for your business, mitigate risks, and build trust with your clients and partners.

Consider seeking legal counsel when drafting contracts, reviewing legal documents, or dealing with complex legal issues. A lawyer can provide invaluable advice, protect your interests, and ensure that your business operates within the bounds of the law. Investing in legal counsel may seem like an added expense, but it's a small price to pay for peace of mind and the long-term success of your solopreneur venture.

The legal landscape may seem like a maze, but with the right knowledge and resources, you can navigate it with confidence. By prioritizing legal compliance and understanding the intricacies of contracts, you can protect your business, build trust with your clients, and create a solid foundation for long-term success. Remember, legal preparedness is not just a matter of legality; it's a strategic advantage that can empower you to thrive in the competitive world of solopreneurship.

ᐧᐧᐧ

Productivity is not about doing more; it's about doing what matters most. Prioritize your tasks, streamline your workflow, and eliminate distractions. Remember, focus is the key to achieving your goals, and time is your most valuable asset.

❥❥❥

FIFTEEN

TAXES DEMYSTIFIED: SIMPLIFYING FINANCES FOR SOLOPRENEURS

Navigating the world of taxes can often feel like traversing a labyrinthine maze, especially for solopreneurs juggling multiple roles and responsibilities. However, understanding the intricacies of taxes is not just a legal obligation; it's a strategic advantage that can empower you to make informed financial decisions, optimize your deductions, and minimize your tax liability. By demystifying taxes, solopreneurs can gain a clearer picture of their financial health, streamline their accounting processes, and ensure compliance with tax regulations.

At the heart of tax simplification lies the concept of record-keeping. Meticulous record-keeping is not just a matter of compliance; it's a window into your business's financial performance. By diligently tracking your income and expenses, you can identify trends, spot potential issues, and make informed decisions about pricing, budgeting, and investment. Utilize accounting software or apps to automate the process, categorize your expenses, and generate reports that provide insights into your financial health.

Understanding the different types of taxes that apply to solopreneurs is crucial. In most jurisdictions, solopreneurs are subject to income tax, self-employment tax, and potentially sales tax. Income tax is levied on your net profits, while self-employment tax covers Social Security and Medicare contributions. Sales tax, on the other hand, is collected on the sale of goods or services and varies depending on the location and nature of your business.

One of the most significant advantages for solopreneurs is the ability to claim deductions for business expenses. These deductions can significantly reduce your taxable income, thereby lowering your tax liability. Eligible expenses can include office supplies, rent, utilities, travel expenses, marketing costs, and even a portion of your home expenses if you have a dedicated workspace. It's essential to keep detailed records of all your business expenses to maximize your deductions.

The concept of estimated taxes can be a source of confusion for many solopreneurs. Unlike traditional employees who have taxes withheld from their paychecks, solopreneurs are responsible for estimating their tax liability and making quarterly payments to the tax authorities. Failure to do so can result in penalties and interest. Consult with a tax professional or use online tax calculators to estimate your tax liability and ensure timely payments.

Tax laws and regulations are constantly evolving, so it's important to stay informed about any changes that might affect your business. Subscribe to newsletters, attend webinars, and consult with tax professionals to ensure you're up-to-date on the latest tax laws. By staying informed, you can avoid costly mistakes and take advantage of new deductions or credits that may be available to you.

Tax planning is not just about minimizing your tax liability; it's about making strategic financial decisions that align with your long-term business goals. This might involve incorporating your business, setting up a retirement plan, or exploring tax-advantaged investment options. Consult with a financial advisor to create a tax plan that optimizes your deductions, minimizes your tax burden, and supports your long-term financial goals.

Technology can be a powerful ally in simplifying your taxes. Numerous accounting software and apps are available that can automate your bookkeeping, track your expenses, generate invoices, and even calculate your estimated taxes. By leveraging technology, you can streamline your financial processes, save time, and reduce the risk of errors.

Seeking professional help can be invaluable when dealing with complex tax issues. A qualified tax professional can help you navigate the intricacies of tax law, maximize your deductions, and ensure compliance with regulations. Consider consulting a tax advisor or accountant, especially if you have a complex business structure or are facing a tax audit.

Remember, taxes are not a burden; they are an investment in your community and your country. By understanding the tax system, keeping meticulous records, claiming legitimate deductions, making estimated tax payments, staying informed about tax laws, planning strategically, leveraging technology, and seeking professional help when needed, you can demystify taxes, simplify your finances, and focus on what you do best: growing your solopreneur venture.

ppp

The legal landscape may seem daunting, but it's a crucial part of the solopreneur's journey. Understand contracts, comply with regulations, and protect your intellectual property. Remember, knowledge is power, and a solid legal foundation is essential for building a sustainable business.

❦❦❦

SIXTEEN

THE ART OF DELEGATION: KNOWING WHEN TO OUTSOURCE

The solopreneur's journey is often a whirlwind of activity, juggling multiple roles, wearing numerous hats, and constantly striving for excellence in every aspect of their business. While this entrepreneurial spirit is commendable, it can also lead to a precarious balancing act, where the sheer volume of tasks threatens to topple the entire enterprise. This is where the art of delegation comes into play, a strategic maneuver that can transform a solopreneur's trajectory from overwhelmed to empowered.

Delegation is not a sign of weakness or an admission of defeat; it's a testament to a solopreneur's wisdom and foresight. It's the recognition that one person cannot, and should not, do it all. By entrusting certain tasks to others, solopreneurs can free up valuable time and mental bandwidth to focus on their core competencies, the activities that truly drive their business forward.

The first step in mastering the art of delegation is to identify tasks that are suitable for outsourcing. Not every task is created equal; some require your unique expertise and attention, while others can be effectively handled by someone else. Start by creating a comprehensive list of all the tasks you perform on a regular basis. Then, categorize them based on their importance, urgency, and your level of expertise. Tasks that are time-consuming, repetitive, or outside your core skillset are prime candidates for delegation.

Once you've identified tasks to delegate, the next step is to find the right people to entrust them to. This could involve hiring freelancers, virtual assistants, or even partnering with other businesses. Consider the specific skills and experience required for each task, as well as the level of trust and communication necessary for a successful collaboration. Don't rush the process; take the time to find individuals or companies that align with your values, understand your vision, and have a proven track record of delivering results.

Clear communication is the cornerstone of successful delegation. Before handing off a task, clearly articulate your expectations, deadlines, and desired outcomes. Provide detailed instructions, share relevant resources, and establish a communication channel for regular updates and feedback. Don't micromanage; trust your collaborators to do their job, but be available to answer questions and provide guidance as needed.

Building trust is a gradual process that requires open communication, transparency, and mutual respect. As you delegate more tasks and build successful collaborations, you'll develop a network of trusted partners who can help you scale your business and achieve your goals. Remember, delegation is not a one-time event; it's an ongoing process that evolves as your business grows and your needs change.

One of the most significant benefits of delegation is the time it frees up for solopreneurs. By offloading non-essential tasks, you can focus your energy and attention on the activities that truly matter – developing new products or services, cultivating client relationships, strategizing for growth, and nurturing your own well-being. This newfound time can also be used for personal pursuits, allowing you to achieve a healthier work-life balance and avoid burnout.

Delegation also allows you to tap into a wider range of expertise and skills. By collaborating with specialists in different fields, you can elevate the quality of your work, offer a wider range of services, and deliver a more comprehensive solution to your clients. This not only enhances your value proposition but also increases your earning potential.

The financial aspect of delegation is often a concern for solopreneurs. While it's true that outsourcing tasks comes with a cost, it's important to view it as an investment, not an expense. By delegating tasks that are not your forte, you can focus on activities that generate higher revenue and ultimately increase your profitability. Moreover, the time and energy saved through delegation can be channeled into other income-generating activities, further boosting your bottom line.

The art of delegation is not just about offloading tasks; it's about empowering others, fostering collaboration, and building a team that can help you achieve your vision. By sharing your knowledge, providing guidance, and recognizing the contributions of your collaborators, you can create a positive and productive work environment that benefits everyone involved.

Knowing when to outsource is a skill that develops with experience. Start small by delegating simple tasks and gradually increase the complexity as you gain confidence in your collaborators. Trust your instincts, communicate clearly, and be open to feedback. By mastering the art of delegation, you can unlock your full potential as a solopreneur, achieve greater success, and build a business that thrives on collaboration and shared expertise.

ᐅᐅᐅ

Taxes may be a necessary evil, but they don't have to be a mystery. Demystify the tax code, keep meticulous records, and seek professional advice when needed. Remember, proactive tax planning can save you money and give you peace of mind.

❧❧❧

SEVENTEEN

THE SOLOPRENEUR'S SANCTUARY: DESIGNING YOUR IDEAL WORKSPACE

The solopreneur's workspace is more than just a physical location; it's a sanctuary, a haven where ideas are born, nurtured, and brought to life. It's a reflection of your personality, your values, and your aspirations. It's a place where you can focus, create, and thrive. Designing your ideal workspace is not just about aesthetics; it's about creating an environment that supports your productivity, creativity, and overall well-being.

The location of your workspace can significantly impact your productivity and mood. Some solopreneurs thrive in the bustling energy of a co-working space, while others prefer the quiet solitude of a home office. Consider your personal preferences, work style, and budget when choosing your location. If you opt for a home office, choose a space that is well-lit, quiet, and free from distractions. If you prefer a co-working space, choose one that aligns with your values and offers the amenities you need, such as high-speed internet, meeting rooms, and a supportive community.

The layout of your workspace is crucial for creating a productive and inspiring environment. Organize your space in a way that promotes flow and minimizes distractions. Consider using a standing desk to improve posture and energy levels, invest in ergonomic furniture to support your body, and declutter your desk to create a clean and organized workspace.

Lighting plays a crucial role in your workspace. Natural light is ideal, as it can boost mood, energy, and productivity. If natural light is limited, invest in full-spectrum light bulbs that mimic natural sunlight. Avoid harsh fluorescent lighting, which can cause eye strain and headaches.

The color palette of your workspace can significantly impact your mood and creativity. Choose colors that inspire you and promote a positive and productive atmosphere. Cool colors, such as blue and green, can promote calmness and focus, while warm colors, such as yellow and orange, can stimulate creativity and energy.

Plants are not just a decorative element; they can also improve air quality, reduce stress, and boost productivity. Consider adding a few plants to your workspace to create a more inviting and relaxing environment.

Personalizing your workspace is essential for making it your own. Add personal touches that reflect your personality, interests, and values. This could include photos, artwork, motivational quotes, or even souvenirs from your travels. Surround yourself with items that inspire you and make you feel good.

In the digital age, technology is an integral part of any workspace. Invest in a reliable computer, a comfortable keyboard and mouse, and a high-quality monitor. Ensure that your internet connection is fast and reliable. Consider using noise-canceling headphones to minimize distractions and create a more focused environment.

Organization is key to a productive workspace. Invest in storage solutions, such as drawers, shelves, and filing cabinets, to keep your workspace tidy and clutter-free. Use a planner or calendar to schedule your tasks and deadlines. Create a system for managing your emails, documents, and other digital files.

The temperature of your workspace can significantly impact your comfort and productivity. Ensure that your workspace is well-ventilated and that the temperature is comfortable. If you're too hot or too cold, it can be difficult to focus and be productive.

The ambiance of your workspace can also affect your mood and creativity. Consider adding elements that create a relaxing and inspiring atmosphere, such as soft music, aromatherapy, or a water feature.

Remember, your workspace is a reflection of you. It's a place where you spend a significant portion of your day, so it's important to create an environment that supports your well-being, inspires your creativity, and fuels your productivity. By taking the time to design your ideal workspace, you're investing in yourself and your business.

Don't be afraid to experiment and try different things. Your workspace is a dynamic space that should evolve as your needs and preferences change. Regularly assess your workspace and make adjustments as needed. By creating a workspace that you love, you'll be more motivated, engaged, and productive, ultimately leading to greater success in your solopreneur journey.

ɊɊɊ

The art of delegation is about more than just offloading tasks; it's about empowering others, leveraging their expertise, and building a team that can help you achieve your vision. Remember, a solopreneur's success is often a collective effort.

❥❥❥

EIGHTEEN

THE POWER OF COMMUNITY: CONNECTING WITH FELLOW SOLOPRENEURS

The solopreneur's path, while paved with autonomy and flexibility, can often feel like a solitary journey. The absence of colleagues, the lack of a traditional team structure, and the weight of independent decision-making can sometimes lead to feelings of isolation and disconnection. However, within this seemingly solitary pursuit lies a powerful remedy: the embrace of community. Connecting with fellow solopreneurs can be a transformative experience, providing a sense of belonging, support, and shared purpose that fuels both personal and professional growth.

Community, in the context of solopreneurship, is a vibrant tapestry woven together by individuals who share a common passion for entrepreneurship, a thirst for knowledge, and a desire to connect with like-minded individuals. It's a space where solopreneurs can come together to share their experiences, exchange ideas, offer support, and celebrate successes. It's a place where the isolation of solo work is replaced with the warmth of camaraderie and the power of collective wisdom.

One of the most significant benefits of connecting with fellow solopreneurs is the sense of belonging it fosters. The solopreneur journey can be fraught with uncertainties, challenges, and self-doubt. Having a community of peers who understand your struggles, celebrate your wins, and offer unwavering support can be a game-changer. It's a reminder that you're not alone in this journey, that there are others who share your passion, your drive, and your dreams.

Collaboration is another powerful outcome of connecting with fellow solopreneurs. By pooling resources, skills, and expertise, solopreneurs can achieve far more than they could on their own. This could involve partnering on projects, sharing marketing efforts, cross-promoting each other's services, or simply offering a listening ear and a fresh perspective. Collaboration not only amplifies your reach and impact but also fosters a spirit of generosity and mutual support within the community.

The exchange of knowledge and ideas is a cornerstone of any thriving community. By connecting with fellow solopreneurs, you gain access to a wealth of experience, insights, and perspectives. This could involve attending workshops, participating in online forums, or simply engaging in casual conversations over coffee. The exchange of knowledge not only broadens your horizons but also sparks new ideas, challenges your assumptions, and inspires innovation.

Mentorship is a natural outgrowth of community. Seasoned solopreneurs can offer invaluable guidance, advice, and support to those who are just starting out. They can share their hard-earned wisdom, help you navigate challenges, and accelerate your growth. Likewise, as you gain experience and expertise, you can pay it forward by mentoring others and contributing to the growth of the community.

Community also provides a platform for celebrating successes and overcoming challenges. By sharing your wins and setbacks with your peers, you can gain valuable insights, receive encouragement, and build resilience. Celebrating milestones together strengthens the bonds within the community and creates a culture of positivity and support.

In today's digital age, connecting with fellow solopreneurs has never been easier. Online communities, forums, and social media groups offer a plethora of opportunities to connect, collaborate, and learn from each other. Attend virtual events, participate in webinars, and engage in online discussions to expand your network and build meaningful relationships.

Co-working spaces are another avenue for connecting with fellow solopreneurs. These shared workspaces not only provide a productive environment but also foster a sense of community and collaboration. By interacting with other solopreneurs in a co-working space, you can exchange ideas, build relationships, and even find potential collaborators or clients.

Don't underestimate the power of in-person connections. Attend industry events, conferences, and meetups to connect with fellow solopreneurs in your area. These face-to-face interactions can lead to deeper connections, stronger relationships, and new opportunities.

Remember, building a strong community takes time, effort, and commitment. Be proactive, reach out to others, and be willing to give as much as you receive. Participate in discussions, offer support, and celebrate the successes of others. By actively engaging in your community, you'll not only reap the benefits of connection, collaboration, and support but also contribute to the growth and vibrancy of the solopreneur ecosystem.

The power of community is a transformative force for solopreneurs. It's a source of inspiration, support, knowledge, and collaboration. By connecting with fellow solopreneurs, you can overcome the isolation of solo work, build lasting relationships, and achieve greater success. So, embrace the power of community, forge meaningful connections, and unlock your full potential as a solopreneur.

ᗡᗡᗡ

*Your workspace is your sanctuary, a reflection of
your creativity and a catalyst for productivity.
Design it with intention, infuse it with inspiration,
and let it fuel your entrepreneurial spirit.
Remember, a well-designed workspace can elevate
your work and enhance your well-being.*

ᗨᗨᗨ

NINETEEN
Celebrating Milestones: Acknowledging Your Successes

The solopreneur's journey is often a whirlwind of activity, marked by relentless pursuit of goals, the constant juggling of tasks, and the unwavering focus on the next milestone. In the midst of this exhilarating yet demanding journey, it's easy to overlook a crucial element: celebrating milestones. Acknowledging and appreciating your successes is not just a feel-good exercise; it's a powerful tool for sustaining motivation, fostering a positive mindset, and propelling yourself towards even greater achievements.

Celebrating milestones is not about vanity or self-indulgence; it's about recognizing the hard work, dedication, and perseverance that have brought you to this point. It's about acknowledging the progress you've made, the challenges you've overcome, and the goals you've achieved. It's a moment to pause, reflect, and appreciate the journey you've embarked upon.

The act of celebration triggers a cascade of positive emotions, such as joy, pride, and satisfaction. These emotions not only boost your mood but also reinforce your sense of self-efficacy, the belief in your own ability to succeed. When you celebrate your milestones, you're sending a message to your subconscious mind that you're capable, you're worthy, and you're on the right track. This positive reinforcement can fuel your motivation, boost your confidence, and propel you towards even greater heights.

Celebrating milestones also serves as a reminder of your purpose and passion. In the daily grind of running a business, it's easy to lose sight of the bigger picture, the reasons why you embarked on this journey in the first place. Taking the time to celebrate your successes allows you to reconnect with your why, reignite your passion, and reaffirm your commitment to your goals.

Moreover, celebrating milestones can be a powerful antidote to burnout. The solopreneur's journey can be isolating and demanding, often leading to exhaustion and a sense of overwhelm. By taking the time to celebrate your wins, you're injecting a dose of positivity and excitement into your routine, breaking the monotony, and recharging your batteries. It's a reminder that your hard work is paying off and that you're making a difference.

Celebrating milestones doesn't have to be an elaborate affair. It can be as simple as taking a moment to reflect on your achievements, treating yourself to a special meal, or sharing your success with friends and family. It could also involve setting aside time for a fun activity, investing in a personal development course, or even taking a well-deserved vacation. The key is to find ways to celebrate that resonate with you and that feel meaningful and rewarding.

Don't wait for major milestones to celebrate. Small wins deserve recognition too. Celebrate every step forward, no matter how small it may seem. Did you land a new client? Celebrate! Did you launch a new product? Celebrate! Did you surpass a revenue goal? Celebrate! By acknowledging and appreciating your small wins, you'll create a positive feedback loop that fuels your motivation and propels you towards even greater achievements.

Sharing your successes with others is another way to amplify the positive impact of celebration. Whether it's with your team, your mentors, your social media followers, or even your competitors, sharing your wins can inspire others, foster a sense of community, and create opportunities for collaboration. It can also attract new clients and partners who are drawn to your positive energy and success.

Celebrating milestones is not just about acknowledging your past achievements; it's also about setting the stage for future success. By taking the time to appreciate your wins, you're reinforcing your commitment to your goals, building momentum, and creating a positive mindset that will propel you towards even greater accomplishments. It's a reminder that you're capable of achieving anything you set your mind to, and that the journey is just as important as the destination.

In the grand tapestry of solopreneurship, celebrating milestones is a vibrant thread that weaves together your past, present, and future. It's a testament to your resilience, your determination, and your unwavering belief in yourself. It's a reminder that you're not just building a business; you're creating a legacy, one milestone at a time.

ᗡᗡᗡ

The power of community is a force to be reckoned with. Connect with fellow solopreneurs, share your experiences, and learn from each other's journeys. Remember, you are not alone in this endeavor, and the collective wisdom of a community can propel you towards greatness.

TWENTY

THE EVER-EVOLVING JOURNEY: EMBRACING CHANGE AND CONTINUED GROWTH

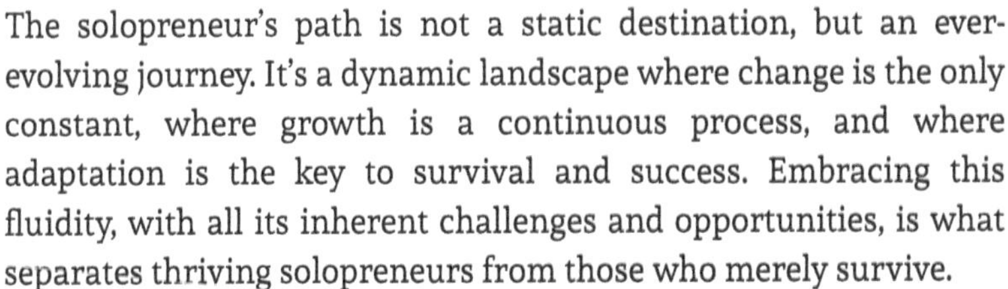

The solopreneur's path is not a static destination, but an ever-evolving journey. It's a dynamic landscape where change is the only constant, where growth is a continuous process, and where adaptation is the key to survival and success. Embracing this fluidity, with all its inherent challenges and opportunities, is what separates thriving solopreneurs from those who merely survive.

Change is the lifeblood of entrepreneurship. It's the force that drives innovation, fuels disruption, and creates new possibilities. The solopreneur who resists change risks stagnation, obsolescence, and ultimately, irrelevance. Embracing change, on the other hand, opens doors to new markets, new technologies, and new ways of doing business. It allows you to stay ahead of the curve, anticipate trends, and adapt your strategies to meet the evolving needs of your clients.

One of the most significant changes a solopreneur faces is the growth of their business. As your venture expands, your roles and responsibilities will shift, requiring you to adapt your skills, knowledge, and mindset. Embrace this growth as an opportunity to learn, evolve, and expand your capabilities. Delegate tasks, build a team, and invest in your professional development to ensure that you're equipped to handle the challenges and opportunities that come with growth.

The technological landscape is constantly evolving, and solopreneurs must stay abreast of the latest trends and tools to remain competitive. This means embracing new technologies, experimenting with different platforms, and continuously learning new skills. Whether it's social media marketing, automation tools, or artificial intelligence, technology can be a powerful ally in streamlining your operations, enhancing your productivity, and reaching a wider audience.

The market is another dynamic force that demands adaptability. Consumer preferences, economic conditions, and industry trends are constantly shifting, requiring solopreneurs to be agile and responsive. Stay informed about the latest market developments, listen to your customers' feedback, and be willing to pivot your strategies to meet the changing needs of the market.

Personal growth is an integral part of the solopreneur's journey. As your business evolves, so too must you. This involves investing in your personal development, acquiring new skills, expanding your knowledge base, and challenging your own assumptions. Read books, attend workshops, seek mentorship, and engage in activities that foster personal growth. By continuously evolving and improving yourself, you'll be better equipped to navigate the challenges and opportunities of solopreneurship.

Embracing change also means being open to new ideas and perspectives. Don't be afraid to challenge the status quo, experiment with different approaches, and learn from your mistakes. The most successful solopreneurs are those who are willing to take risks, think outside the box, and constantly seek new ways to improve their business.

Resilience is a key component of embracing change. Setbacks and failures are inevitable on the entrepreneurial journey. However, it's how you respond to these challenges that will determine your success. Embrace setbacks as learning opportunities, adapt your strategies, and keep moving forward. Remember, every failure is a stepping stone on the path to success.

Building a strong support network is crucial for navigating the ever-changing landscape of solopreneurship. Surround yourself with mentors, peers, and advisors who can offer guidance, support, and encouragement. Join online communities, attend networking events, and connect with other solopreneurs who understand the unique challenges and rewards of this journey. By building a strong support system, you'll have a network of people to lean on when times get tough, to celebrate your successes with, and to learn from.

The ever-evolving journey of solopreneurship is not for the faint of heart. It requires courage, adaptability, resilience, and an insatiable thirst for learning. But for those who embrace the challenges and opportunities of this dynamic landscape, the rewards are immeasurable. The freedom to pursue your passion, the satisfaction of creating something meaningful, the ability to make a difference in the world, and the potential for financial independence are just a few of the many benefits of this fulfilling path.

Remember, the solopreneur's journey is not a linear path; it's a winding road filled with unexpected twists and turns. Embrace the uncertainty, celebrate the change, and never stop learning and growing. By cultivating a growth mindset, staying informed about market trends, adapting to new technologies, investing in your personal development, and building a strong support network, you can navigate the ever-evolving journey of solopreneurship with confidence, resilience, and joy.

▷▷▷

Celebrating milestones is not just about acknowledging your successes; it's about fueling your motivation, reinforcing your self-belief, and creating a positive feedback loop that propels you towards even greater achievements. Remember, every step forward deserves recognition, and every victory is a testament to your resilience and determination.

▷▷▷

TWENTY-ONE
SUMMARY

The solopreneur's odyssey is a thrilling adventure, filled with challenges, triumphs, and endless opportunities for growth. It's a journey fueled by passion, resilience, and an unwavering belief in one's dreams.

The spark that ignites this odyssey often begins with a deep introspection, a quest to uncover one's entrepreneurial passion. This involves exploring interests, reflecting on past experiences, and stepping outside of comfort zones. Once that spark is ignited, it's time to take a leap of faith, confronting fears and embracing the uncertainties that lie ahead. Overcoming these fears requires a shift in perspective, reframing them as compasses guiding personal and professional growth.

With passion and resilience as your guiding lights, it's time to craft a blueprint for your dreams, a comprehensive business plan that outlines your vision, strategies, and financial projections. This plan serves as a roadmap, guiding your decisions and ensuring that your business stays on course.

While the solopreneur's path may seem solitary, it's far from it. Building a strong support network of mentors, peers, and loved ones is crucial for navigating challenges, celebrating successes, and fostering personal and professional growth. This network provides a safe space for sharing experiences, exchanging ideas, and receiving guidance and encouragement.

Mastering the juggle between work and life is an ongoing challenge for solopreneurs. Setting boundaries, managing time and energy effectively, and prioritizing self-care are essential for maintaining a healthy balance and avoiding burnout. Technology can be a powerful ally in this endeavor, streamlining operations and enhancing productivity.

Money matters are a critical aspect of solopreneurship. Financial planning, budgeting, and understanding taxes are essential for ensuring the long-term sustainability of your business. This involves separating personal and business finances, tracking income and expenses, managing cash flow, and making informed investment decisions.

Attracting and engaging clients is the lifeblood of any solopreneur venture. Crafting a compelling brand identity, creating valuable content, leveraging social media, and building strong client relationships are key to establishing a loyal customer base and growing your business.

Technology plays a pivotal role in the solopreneur's journey. A robust tech toolkit, including a reliable computer, cloud storage, a professional website, email marketing platforms, social media tools, project management software, communication tools, accounting software, and cybersecurity measures, can significantly enhance productivity and streamline operations.

Building strong relationships with clients is essential for long-term success. Understanding their needs, communicating effectively, building trust, exceeding expectations, and fostering genuine connections are key to creating loyal advocates who will not only continue to do business with you but also refer you to others.

The solopreneur's path is not without its setbacks. However, resilience is the key to bouncing back from these challenges. Cultivating a growth mindset, building a strong support system, prioritizing self-care, adapting to change, and learning from mistakes are essential for overcoming adversity and achieving success.

A growth mindset is a cornerstone of solopreneurship. It's a belief in one's ability to learn and grow, a willingness to embrace challenges, and a commitment to continuous improvement. By fostering a thirst for learning, seeking feedback, and surrounding yourself with like-minded individuals, you can unlock your full potential and achieve extraordinary results.

Creating a unique brand identity is essential for standing out in the crowded marketplace. Your brand is more than just a logo; it's the essence of your business, the values you embody, and the promises you make to your customers. By crafting a compelling brand story, developing a consistent visual identity and brand voice, and delivering on your brand promise, you can create a loyal following and establish yourself as a leader in your field.

Optimizing your workflow is crucial for maximizing productivity and achieving your goals. This involves prioritizing tasks, managing your time effectively, automating repetitive tasks, utilizing the right tools, creating a dedicated workspace, taking breaks, delegating tasks, and maintaining a healthy work-life balance.

Understanding the legal landscape is essential for protecting your business and building trust with clients and partners. This involves understanding contracts, complying with regulations, protecting your intellectual property, and prioritizing privacy and data protection.

Taxes can be a complex and daunting aspect of solopreneurship. However, by understanding the different types of taxes, keeping meticulous records, claiming legitimate deductions, making estimated tax payments, staying informed about tax laws, and seeking professional help when needed, you can simplify your finances and minimize your tax liability.

The art of delegation is a valuable skill for solopreneurs. By identifying tasks that can be outsourced and finding the right people to entrust them to, you can free up valuable time and mental bandwidth to focus on your core competencies and grow your business.

Your workspace is more than just a physical location; it's a sanctuary that reflects your personality and supports your productivity. Designing your ideal workspace involves considering factors such as location, layout, lighting, color palette, personalization, technology, organization, temperature, and ambiance.

Connecting with fellow solopreneurs is a powerful way to combat isolation, gain support, exchange ideas, and collaborate on projects. Online communities, forums, co-working spaces, and industry events offer a plethora of opportunities to connect with like-minded individuals and build lasting relationships.

Celebrating milestones is essential for maintaining motivation, fostering a positive mindset, and propelling yourself towards even greater achievements. By acknowledging your successes, reconnecting with your purpose, and sharing your wins with others, you can create a positive feedback loop that fuels your entrepreneurial spirit.

Embracing change and continued growth are essential for thriving in the ever-evolving world of solopreneurship. By adapting to new technologies, staying informed about market trends, investing in personal development, and building a strong support network, you can navigate the challenges and opportunities of this dynamic landscape with confidence and resilience.

❧❧❧

Citation And References

This book represents the culmination of extensive research and meticulous analysis, incorporating a diverse range of sources, including numerous books, scholarly studies, and personal experiences. Additionally, I have scoured various websites to gather relevant information and data essential for the compilation of this work. I have taken every precaution to ensure the accuracy of the information presented and have diligently cited all sources to acknowledge their contributions.

Despite these efforts, the possibility of inadvertent errors remains. I deeply value the insights of my readers and appreciate any feedback that can help identify and rectify such inaccuracies. I encourage you to bring any discrepancies to my attention.

Your feedback is not only welcome but crucial, as it will aid in correcting current editions and enhancing the content of future ones. I am committed to maintaining the highest standards of accuracy and reliability in my work and thank you for your support and understanding.

Additionally, I firmly uphold the principle of freedom of speech and expression as guaranteed under Article 19(1)(a) of the Constitution of India, and I respect the diverse viewpoints and expressions of all readers.

ppp

Other Books Of The Author

1. Empowering Minds: A Journey into Women's Self-Discovery and Power
2. The Dynamics of Motivation: Catalyzing Thought into Action
3. Meditation and Mental Well Being: The Path to Inner Peace and Clarity
4. The Psychology of Child Education: Nurturing Future Generations
5. Ethical Enlightenment: A Modern Guide to Living with Integrity
6. Voices of Empowerment: Stories of Women Rising Against Odds
7. Social Psychology in Everyday Life: Understanding Human Connections
8. The Essence of Motivational Speaking: Inspiring Change in Others
9. Balancing Acts: Women, Work, and the Will to Lead
10. Guiding with Grace: Raising Children with Compassion and Awareness
11. The Power of Positive Aging: Embracing Life After Fifty
12. Building Resilient Communities: Social Work in Action
13. The Ethical Educator: Principles for Teaching and Learning
14. From Insight to Impact: Social Psychology for a Better World
15. The Ethics of Empathy: A Guide to Ethical Living
16. The Science of Empowering the Self: Navigating Life's Challenges with Psychological Wisdom
17. The Mindful Conscious Leader: Meditation Techniques for Modern Management
18. Pioneering Spirit: Women's Pathways to Leadership and Empowerment
19. Feeling to Healing: The Role of Emotional Intelligence in Child Development
20. Transformative Talks and Words of Inspiration: Insights into Motivational Oratory

21. Green Ethics: A Path to Sustainable Living
22. Spiritual Integrity: Navigating Life with Moral Compassion
23. Clean Living, Clean Society: The Ethics of Cleanliness
24. Patriotic Spirits: Building a Nation on Positive Attitudes
25. Innovative Integrity & Vibrant Visions: The Ethical and Entrepreneurial Spirit of Gujarat
26. Youthful Visions, Endless Possibilities: Inspiring Ethics and Motivation in Children
27. Living Your Legacy: How to Motivate Others by Living Your Values
28. Secret of Healing Conversations: Ethical Practices in Counselling and Therapy
29. Creative Kindness: Crafting a Life of Compassion and Creativity
30. The Power of Appreciation: How Gratitude Can Transform Your Relationships
31. Bhagavad-Gita: Messages
32. Science of Art: The New Frontier of Fashion Modernism
33. Vivekananda's Virtues: A Blueprint for Modern Living
34. Empower Her: Navigating the Path to Women's Entrepreneurship
35. The Boundless Classroom: Innovations in Global Education
36. The Language of Leadership: Communicating with Authenticity and Impact
37. The Warrior's Mantra: Deciphering the Hanuman Chalisa
38. Echoes of Empathy: Transformative Stories of Social Service
39. Artful Living: Cultivating Creativity in Your Daily Routine
40. Finding Your Why: Discovering Your Passions and Charting Your Course
41. The Role of Social Media in Shaping Self-Esteem and Interpersonal Relationships among Adolescents
42. Karma's Tapestry: Weaving a Life of Selfless Service
43. Altruistic Alchemy: Transforming Lives Through Giving
44. The Blueprint of Pro-Activeness and Productivity: Crafting Habits for Success
45. The Simplicity with Grounded Wisdom: Embracing Authenticity

in a Complex World

46. Secret of Solopreneur's Odyssey: Navigating the Path to Self-Employment
47. Exploring Tapestry of Peace: Global Perspectives on Harmony
48. The Art and Actions of Connection: Mastering Communication for Impact
49. She Governs and at the Helm: Strategies for Political Empowerment
50. Rising Above and Rising with Grace: A Woman's Roadmap to Career Mastery
51. The Effect of Networking & Connectedness: Building Strategic Alliances for Women
52. Beyond his Barriers: Women Thriving in Male-Dominated Fields
53. Secret of Inner Compass: Navigating Life with Intuition
54. Creative & Pro-Active Muses: A Celebration of Women in the Arts
55. Unburdened: The Art of Releasing the Past
56. Amplified Voices: Speeches of Women that Astonished the World
57. Secret of Manifesting Dreams: A Woman's Guide to Intentional Living
58. Ethics and Value Based Education: Reimagining Japan's School System
59. The Moral Compass Curriculum: A Holistic Approach
60. Tech with Heart: Integrating Ethics into Digital Learning
61. Honoring Virtue: Recognizing Ethical Excellence in Education
62. Raising Good Humans: A Guide to Character Development
63. The Spark Within: Nurturing Creativity in Children
64. The Teenager Whisperer: Navigating Adolescence with Grace
65. Igniting a Passion for Learning: Inspiring Lifelong Curiosity
66. The Habit Lab: Cultivating Positive Behaviors in Children
67. Seeds of Empathy: Fostering Compassion in Young Hearts
68. The Reading Revolution: Inspiring a Love of Books in Children
69. The Learning Brain: Unlocking the Secrets of Student Success
70. Teaching for All: Differentiated Instruction Strategies
71. The Time Alchemist: Mastering Time Management for Peak Performance

72. The Resilience Factor: Transforming Setbacks into Stepping Stones

73. The Healing Touch of Nature: An Introduction to Naturopathy

74. Echoes of the Past: Healing Through Past Life Regression

75. The Spiritual Healer's Handbook: Exploring Energy Medicine

76. Crystal Clarity: Unveiling the Power of Gemstones

77. The Dream Weaver's Guide: Decoding the Language of Dreams

78. Emotional Alchemy: Transforming Pain into Power

79. Sonic Serenity: Harnessing Sound for Stress Relief

80. The Entrepreneur's Playbook: Launching Your Business with Confidence

81. Productivity Unleashed: Time Management Strategies for Entrepreneurs

82. The Problem Solver's Toolkit: Creative Solutions for Business Challenges

83. The Future is Now: Emerging Trends in Business

84. The Curious Explorer: A Child's Guide to Scientific Discovery

85. Digital Pioneers: Empowering Kids in the Tech World

86. The Young Philosopher's Guide: Exploring Life's Big Questions

87. Finding Your Voice: Communication Skills for Confident Kids

88. Nature's Playground: A Child's Guide to Outdoor Adventure

89. Growing a Greener Tomorrow: A Guide to Tree Planting & Conservation

90. Driving with Purpose: Ethical Choices on the Road

91. The Healing Touch: Cultivating Compassion in Healthcare

92. Navigating the Digital Landscape: Ethics in the Age of Social Media

93. The Ethical Closet: A Guide to Sustainable Fashion

94. The Mindful Voyager: Sustainable Travel Practices

95. The Feminine Divine: Honoring the Goddesses of India

96. Sacred Sounds: Chanting Your Way to Inner Peace

97. The Yoga Path: Uniting with the Divine Within

98. Rites of Passage: Creating Meaningful Ceremonies

99. The Chakra System: A Map of Inner Transformation

100. Spiritual Sangha: Finding Community through Satsang and

Bhajan

101. Pilgrimage of the Soul: Spiritual Journeys in India

ppp

Dr. Minakshi Bansal
Social Activist
Ahmedabad, Gujarat, Bharat
minakshiindiag20@yahoo.com

❦❦❦

|| LOKAHA SAMASTHAHA SUKHINO BHAVANTU ||

॥ ॥ ॥